TOP OF THE **FOOD CHAIN**

LION

KILLER KING OF THE PLAINS

LOUISE SPILSBURY

WINDMILL
BOOKS
New York

Published in 2014 by Windmill Books, An Imprint of Rosen Publishing
29 East 21st Street, New York, NY 10010

Produced for Windmill by Calcium Creative Ltd
Editor for Calcium Creative Ltd: Sarah Eason
US Editor: Sara Howell
Designers: Paul Myerscough and Keith Williams

Photo credits: Shutterstock: Aragami12345s 29b, BasPhoto 13t, Riaan van den Berg 14, 28, Bjogroet 5b, Clickit 12, Neal Cooper 8, Boris Diakovsky 6, EastVillage Images 10, 29t, Eric Isselee 16, 21b, Jarp2 17b, LeonP 4, Elize Lotter 26, Oleksandr Lysenko 21t, MJStone 19b, Anna Omelchenko 5t, Parris Blue Productions 19t, PhotoSky 27, Stu Porter cover, J Reineke 9t, 18, Louie Schoeman 9b, Peter Schwarz 11t, Nickolay Stanev 17t, Johan Swanepoel 20, 23t, 25t, Pal Teravagimov 11b, Mogens Trolle 7, 13b, 15, 24, Sergey Uryadnikov 25b, Xtreme Safari Inc. 22, Oleg Znamenskiy 1, 23b.

Library of Congress Cataloging-in-Publication Data

Spilsbury, Louise.
  Lion : killer king of the plains / by Louise Spilsbury.
      pages cm. — (Top of the food chain)
  Includes index.
  ISBN 978-1-61533-740-8 (library binding) — ISBN 978-1-61533-797-2 (pbk.) — ISBN 978-1-61533-798-9 (6-pack)
  1. Lion—Juvenile literature. 2. Predatory animals—Juvenile literature. I. Title.
  QL737.C23S5845 2014
  599.757—dc23
                                    2013002093

Manufactured in the United States of America

CPSIA Compliance Information: Batch #BS13WM: For Further Information contact Windmill Books, New York, New York at 1-866-478-0556

CONTENTS

GRASSLANDS KING

The lion is king of the grasslands in Africa. Grasslands are hot, dry **habitats** that are covered with long grasses and patches of thorny trees and bushes. Lions are **predators** that catch and eat zebras, giraffes, and other large animals.

A **food chain** shows the living things that eat each other within a habitat. Grass plants are at the bottom of most grassland food chains. They make their own food using **energy** from the Sun. Plants are one of the few living things that can make their own food. Grazing animals, such as zebras and wildebeests, eat the grasses and predators such as lions eat the grazing animals.

Lions are the largest predators on the African grasslands.

*Mighty lions prowl among the long, dry grasses of the grasslands searching for **prey**.*

Lions are the only predators that can take on a huge adult giraffe.

Links in the Food Chain

Lions are at the top of their grassland food chains. One food chain begins with plants called acacia trees. Giraffes eat leaves from the acacia tree and then lions eat the giraffes. No animals eat the mighty lion. That's why it is at the top of the food chain!

Lions are large, powerful cats. Like tigers, leopards, and other big, wild cats, lions have long bodies and long tails. They are covered in short, thick fur. Lions have round heads with large eyes, upright ears, and long whiskers around their mouths. They are the only cats that have tufts at the end of their tails.

Although wild cats look similar to pet cats, you wouldn't want to risk petting one! An adult male lion can be 3 feet (1 m) tall and almost 10 feet (3 m) long from its nose to the tip of its tail. That's the length of a small car!

Like pet cats, lions spend a lot of time lying around!

KILLER FACT

A lion's mane is a collar of long, stiff, wiry fur around its neck. The mane makes a male lion look even bigger and scarier than he really is. When a male fights, the mane helps to **protect** its throat from an enemy's sharp teeth.

In fights with other lions, a lion's mane protects it from bites to the throat or the neck.

Another reason lions are at the top of the food chain is that their bodies are built to kill. Along with being big, lions are very muscular animals with **flexible** bodies that can twist and bend. Their powerful back legs are built for running, jumping, and climbing. They can jump and pounce both high and far!

Lions have powerful muscles in their chest and front legs, too. These give them the strength they need to grab and hold onto large, struggling prey. Lions also use their muscles to force prey down to the ground so they can kill it. Lions use their daggerlike teeth and sharp claws to rip into and tear flesh.

Lions can leap up to 12 feet (4 m) high and 40 feet (12 m) across the ground.

KILLER FACT

A lion's mighty paws are deadly weapons. Lions often kill prey by leaping at it and breaking the animal's neck with a swipe of its heavy paw. One blow from a lion's paw is heavy enough to break a zebra's back.

A lion's paw has soft pads. These pads help make the lion's movements quiet and help it sneak up on prey.

Lions climb trees using their claws to dig into the trunks for support.

9

A LION'S PRIDE

Most wild cats live and hunt alone, but lions are unusual in that they live in groups. A group of lions is called a **pride**. An average pride of lions has around 12 to 15 members, but some prides have up to 40 lions or more.

A pride works together as a team. Each member of the team has a job to do. Males protect and guard the pride. Females do most of the hunting and care for the cubs. The pride's teamwork is another reason lions are at the top of the food chain. Together, lions can fight off packs of **hyenas** that try to steal their food. As a team they can also hunt and kill animals that are far bigger than themselves, such as wildebeests.

An average pride of lions might have two adult males, five lionesses, four young lions, and three or four cubs.

Male lions are fierce and strong because it is their job to protect the rest of the pride.

Links in the Food Chain

Wildebeests, or gnu, are a type of antelope. Adult wildebeests can be up to 4.5 feet (1.4 m) tall. They travel in large herds and eat grass all the time.

A wildebeest's horns look dangerous, but its usual response to danger is to run away quickly.

A pride of lions lives and hunts in a special part of their habitat, called a **territory**. This is an area where there are plenty of prey animals for lions to hunt. The males in a pride rule this territory and will stop at nothing to keep other lions from hunting there.

Male lions patrol their territory, looking out for any intruders. They scratch marks into the ground with their claws and spray strong-smelling **urine** around the edges of the territory. They roar loudly to warn lions from other prides to keep out. If an intruder enters the territory, the males try to scare and chase it away. If that doesn't work, the lions attack.

Lions choose land for their territory that has pools of water to drink from.

A lion's roar can be heard up to 5 miles (8 km) away!

Zebras live in herds to make sure there are plenty of eyes on the lookout for lions.

Links in the Food Chain

Just as people have unique fingerprints, each zebra has its own special set of stripes. Some scientists think the stripes make it harder for lions to **focus** on one single zebra when the whole herd runs away. This makes it much harder for the lions to catch one of the zebras.

13

HIDDEN KILLER

A lion's sandy brown fur is like the color of the baked soil and the dry grasses of the grasslands where it lives. This **camouflage** helps lions to blend in with the grassy background while they are hunting. Lions are so big that they are too heavy to run quickly for long, so they often use camouflage to help them sneak up on prey.

When lions see a prey animal, they slowly sneak up on it. The soft pads on their paws help the lions to move silently. If a prey animal looks around, the lions freeze until it looks away again. When they are close enough, the lions chase or pounce on the animal.

Lions sometimes use their camouflage to lie in grasses near a watering hole until a prey animal comes to drink!

KILLER FACT

When a lion gets close enough to its prey, it suddenly launches itself from the grasses and sprints fast. Lions can run at 40 miles per hour (65 km/h), but they can only hold this top speed for a distance of around 300 feet (100 m).

Lions must get close to their prey before charging because they cannot run fast for long.

TEAM HUNTING

Lionesses do most of the hunting. When a team of lionesses spots a herd of prey animals, these skilled hunters often split into two groups. One group runs out to scare and chase the prey in one direction. The other group lies in wait to catch the terrified prey as it runs toward them.

Sometimes lionesses form a wide circle and surround a herd. Then the lionesses work together to corner and kill one animal, often a weak or old member of the herd. Lionesses also form a line and run to chase prey toward a dead end, such as a watering hole, where there is no escape.

This lioness is about to lead her team in an attack on a herd of wildebeests.

Lionesses work as a superbly organized team to hunt prey.

Links in the Food Chain

Gazelles have big, bulging eyes that are positioned on the sides of their heads. This helps them to see far and wide around them, so they can spot predators moving in on them from the side and behind.

Gazelles live in large herds of up to several hundred animals.

17

SIGNAL SKILLS

When lionesses hunt together, they often use sounds to "talk" to each other. They make soft grunting or growling sounds to keep in **contact** with each other. While walking through long grass, the lionesses hold their tails upright so other lionesses can find or follow them.

Lionesses also use signals. When a lioness opens her mouth slightly, pricks up her ears, and holds her tail upright it means she has found and is looking at prey. If she lashes her tail during a hunt, it tells the others she's about to go in for the kill. When catching prey, lions use their sharp claws to stop it from escaping.

Lionesses often grunt to "talk" to each other while hunting.

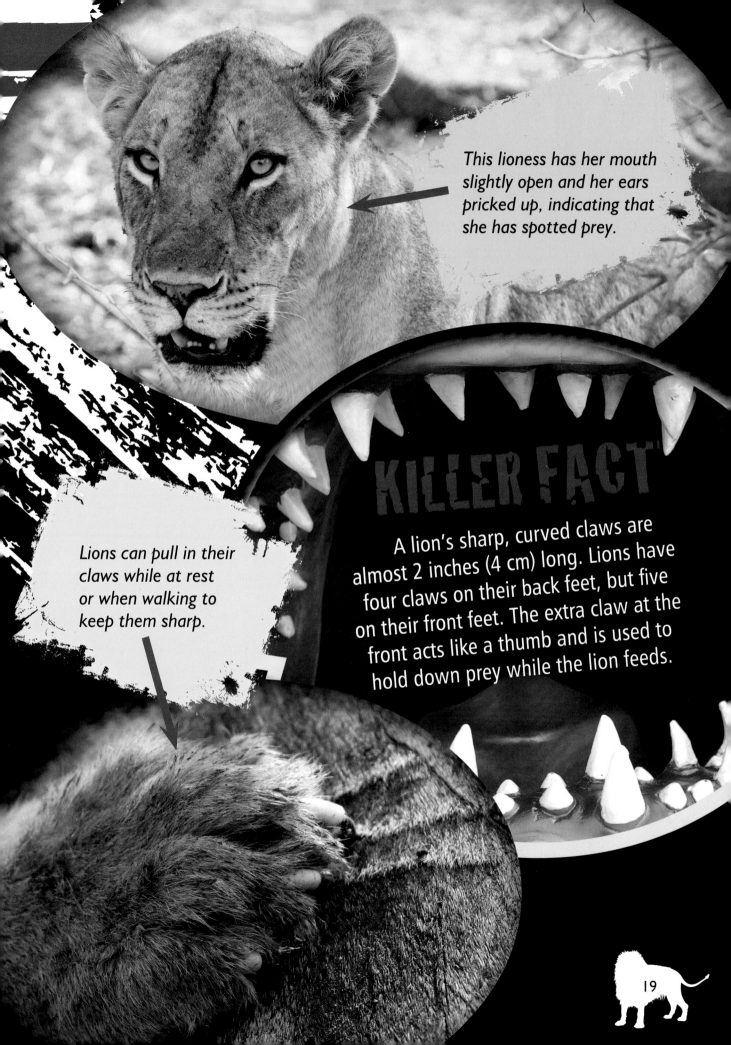

This lioness has her mouth slightly open and her ears pricked up, indicating that she has spotted prey.

Lions can pull in their claws while at rest or when walking to keep them sharp.

KILLER FACT

A lion's sharp, curved claws are almost 2 inches (4 cm) long. Lions have four claws on their back feet, but five on their front feet. The extra claw at the front acts like a thumb and is used to hold down prey while the lion feeds.

SUPER SENSES

Lions use their super **senses** of hearing and sight to help them hunt in dim light at dusk and dawn, and also at night. Their ears can hear prey up to 1 mile (2 km) away.

Pet cats have **pupils** that are shaped like slits, but lions have big, round pupils. The round pupil allows lots of light to filter into the eye at night, which gives the lion good night vision. A white circle below the eye helps to reflect light into the eyes, and a reflective coating at the back of the eye reflects even moonlight. This makes lion eyes an amazing six times more sensitive to light than human eyes.

Lions swivel and twist their upright ears in different directions to pinpoint exactly where sounds are coming from.

KILLER FACT

Lions and other cats have a special part in the roof of their mouths called a "Jacobson's **organ**," which helps them to smell. Lions open their lips when smelling something to draw air over the organ.

Lions open their mouths like this to take in scents over their Jacobson's organ.

Lions can see almost as well at night as humans can during the day!

Once a prey animal is caught, lions kill it immediately. Sometimes they kill the prey by biting into its throat to crush its windpipe. Other times they leap on the prey's back and bite into the back of its neck to break the backbone. When hunting in groups, one lion clamps its mouth over the prey's nose and mouth while the other lions hold it down.

After a kill, all the lions in a pride run to catch up with the hunters. The adult male lions from the pride feed first, while the females growl grumpily until they get their turn to eat. The cubs have to wait until last.

A lion's tongue is covered with rough spines that scrape skin off meat and meat off bones.

KILLER FACT

Lions have 30 sharp, deadly teeth. The four large and pointed **canine** teeth are up to 3 inches (7 cm) long. These teeth hold prey tightly and bite and kill it. Lions open and close their other teeth on flesh like a pair of scissors, slicing off chunks of meat that they then swallow whole.

A lion's teeth are perfectly designed for killing and eating its prey.

After eating a big meal, lions spend a day or two resting and digesting their food. Then they are ready to hunt and feed again.

When lion cubs are born, they are helpless. Their eyes do not open for two weeks and they cannot run for a month. The cubs' coats are spotted at first, to help camouflage them in the grass. The camouflage hides the cubs from predators such as hyenas and leopards.

At about six weeks old, cubs begin to learn to hunt. They build up strength and skill by chasing, **stalking**, and wrestling each other. Their mother brings the cubs small or injured animals to chase, to teach them how to hunt and kill. From around a year old, the cubs join in hunts.

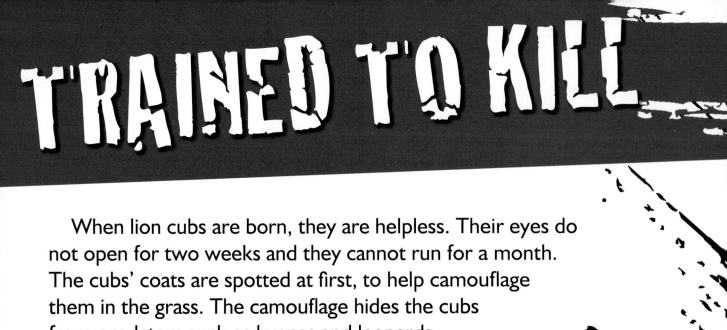

All the members of a pride help to watch over lion cubs and will defend them fiercely from attack.

Links in the Food Chain

Lion cubs also learn to follow vultures that they see circling in the sky. The vultures lead lions to **carcasses**. Lions are great **scavengers**, and as much as 40 percent of their food comes from animals that are already dead or food stolen from other predators.

Vultures spend a lot of their time soaring around looking for food.

*Mother lions teach cubs to hunt, kill, and eat **mammals**.*

LION DANGERS

Lions are at the top of their food chain, but they face danger from people. Today, the biggest threat to lions is the loss of their habitat. In Africa, people are taking over more and more land to use for farming or to build homes on. Without land to live and hunt on, lions are at risk. Many of Africa's lions now live in **reserves** rather than in the wild.

Farmers and herders kill lions to protect their livestock. Some countries still allow hunters to shoot lions for sport, too. Even lions that live in reserves are not completely safe. They may be killed by **poachers** or villagers if they roam too far beyond the borders of the reserve.

When people take over African grasslands, there is less land for herds of grazing animals to live, which means fewer prey for lions to eat.

Droughts in Africa are increasing so more farmers are keeping tough goats instead of cattle.

Links in the Food Chain

Many African farmers raise goats for milk and meat. Goats are cheap, tough animals that can survive very dry summers better than cattle. When there are fewer grazing animals in an area, some lions kill goats and other livestock to eat instead.

NO MORE LIONS?

If the predators at the top of a food chain disappear, the chain begins to fail. Predators keep herds of grazing animals healthy because they remove sick and weak animals. Lions also provide food for other animals. When a lion makes a kill, it often leaves behind some of the prey's body, which is then food for scavengers such as vultures.

Without lions, the numbers of animals that they eat would increase too much. This can be a disaster. For example, if there were no lions, the number of giraffes would quickly grow. Too many giraffes would eat too many trees and shrubs. Soon, the giraffes would run out of food and starve. Fewer giraffes would mean less food for other predators such as cheetahs, and they would soon starve to death, too.

It is important to have predators such as lions at the top of the food chain.

These lions live in a wildlife reserve where they are safe from harm.

Links in the Food Chain

Giraffes are the tallest mammals in the world. They use their long legs and neck and 20-inch-(50 cm) long tongue to reach leaves high in treetops that few other animals can reach.

Being tall helps giraffes reach food and spot lions!

GLOSSARY

camouflage (KA-muh-flahj) When something is hard to see because its coloring blends into the surroundings.

canine (KAY-nyn) Long, pointed teeth in a predator's upper jaw.

carcasses (KAR-kus-ez) Dead animals.

contact (KON-takt) Touching, to touch.

energy (EH-ner-jee) The power to live, grow, and move.

flexible (FLEK-sih-bul) Able to easily move.

focus (FOH-kis) To concentrate on.

food chain (FOOD CHAYN) Living things connected because they are one another's food.

habitats (HA-buh-tatz) Natural environments in which a living thing is found.

hyenas (hy-EE-nuhz) A type of wild dog that lives in Africa.

mammals (MA-mulz) Animals that have fur or hair, give birth to live young, and feed their young on milk from the mother's body.

organ (AWR-gun) A part inside the body that does a job.

poachers (POH-cherz) People who hunt illegally, for example hunting animals in a reserve.

predators (PREH-duh-terz) Animals that hunt other animals for food.

prey (PRAY) Animals that are hunted by other animals for food.

pride (PRYD) A group of lions that live together.

protect (pruh-TEKT) Keep safe.

pupils (PYOO-pulz) Black holes in the center of the eyes that lets light into the eyes.

reserves (rih-ZURVZ) Areas of protected land where animals such as lions can live safely.

scavengers (SKA-ven-jurz) Animals that feed on dead or rotting animals.

senses (SEN-sez) The parts of the body that detect particular things in the environment, such as light, chemicals, and sound waves. The senses give a living thing information about the world around it.

stalking (STOK-ing) Chasing or approaching prey silently and secretly.

territory (TER-uh-tor-ee) An area of ground that a pack of lions are prepared to defend against other lions.

urine (YUR-un) Waste and excess water from the body.

FURTHER READING

Carney, Elizabeth. *National Geographic Kids Everything*
Big Cats: Pictures to Purr About and Info to Make You Roar!
Des Moines, IA: National Geographic Children's Books, 2011.

Joubert, Beverly, and Dereck Joubert. *Face to Face with Lions*.
Face to Face with Animals. Des Moines, IA: National Geographic
Children's Books, 2010.

Meinking, Mary. *Lion vs. Gazelle*. Predator vs. Prey.
Chicago, IL: Heinemann-Raintree, 2011.

Spilsbury, Richard, and Louise Spilsbury. *Lion Prides*. Animal Armies.
New York: PowerKids Press, 2013.

WEBSITES

For web resources related to the subject of this book, go to:
www.windmillbooks.com/weblinks and select this book's title.

INDEX